HOUGHTON MIFFLIN HARCOURT

Texas JOURNEYS

Program Authors

James F. Baumann · David J. Chard · Jamal Cooks
J. David Cooper · Russell Gersten · Marjorie Lipson
Lesley Mandel Morrow · John J. Pikulski · Héctor H. Rivera
Mabel Rivera · Shane Templeton · Sheila W. Valencia
Catherine Valentino · MaryEllen Vogt

Consulting Author
Irene Fountas

HOUGHTON MIFFLIN HARCOURT
School Publishers

Cover illustration by Claudine Gevry.

Printed in the U.S.A.

ISBN 10:   0-54-724082-1
ISBN 13:   978-0-54-724082-4

456789 - 0868 – 18 17 16 15 14 13 12 11 10
4500226924

Hello, Reader!

What happens to living things as they grow? That's what the stories in this book are about. You will meet animals and children who are learning new things. You will even meet a silly pig who wonders if a piece of cheese and a dog bone will help his tree grow.

As you read, the number of words you know grows, too! Read on!

Sincerely,

The Authors

Watch Us Grow

Big Idea Living things change as they grow.

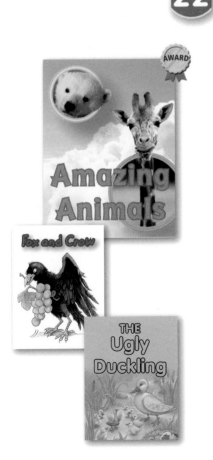

Watch Us Grow

unit 5

Big Idea

Living things change as they grow.

Selections

Read Together | **I Read** | **Read Together**

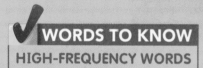

✔ WORDS TO KNOW
HIGH-FREQUENCY WORDS

told

night

pretty

window

thought

better

turned

saw

Vocabulary
Reader

Context
Cards

TEKS 1.3H identify/read high-frequency
words; **ELPS** 1F use accessible language to
learn new language; 3B expand/internalize initial
English vocabulary

10

Words to Know

Read Together

● **Read each** Context Card.

● **Choose two blue words.**
Use them in sentences.

1
told
He **told** the class the
name of the tree.

2
night
The buds open in the
day and close at **night**.

3 pretty

This is a **pretty** wide tree trunk!

4 window

The big tree is very close to the **window**.

5 thought

The man **thought** about planting a tree.

6 better

The tree got **better** when he watered it.

7 turned

The leaves **turned** orange in the fall.

8 saw

They **saw** many apples on the trees.

11

TEKS **1.3H** identify/read high-frequency words; **1.6D** categorize words; **1.14D** use text features to locate information; **ELPS** **3D** speak using content-area vocabulary ; **4D** use prereading supports to comprehend texts

Background

✓ **WORDS TO KNOW**   Life in a Tree

There is a tree outside my window.
One day, I saw birds and squirrels
in the tree. That night I thought I
would take another look. I turned on
a flashlight to see better. I saw an
owl in the tree. I told my dad, "That
tree is a pretty busy place!"

leaves

branch

trunk

bark

Find the parts of a tree in the picture.
Tell a partner what other parts you know.

Comprehension

Read Together

✓ **TARGET SKILL** Story Structure

Remember that a story has different parts. **Characters** are the people and animals in a story. The **setting** is when and where a story takes place. The **plot** is the order of story events. The events are often about a problem and how the characters solve it.

> **What is the problem?**
> **How can it be solved?**

After reading **The Tree**, tell who is in it, where they are, and what they do.

Characters	Setting
Plot	

Read Together

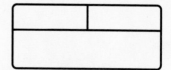 **WORDS TO KNOW**

told	thought
night	better
pretty	turned
window	saw

✔ **TARGET SKILL**

Story Structure Tell the setting, character, and events in a story.

✔ **TARGET STRATEGY**

Analyze/Evaluate Tell how you feel about the text, and why.

GENRE

A **fantasy** story could not happen in real life.

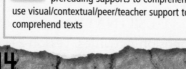 **TEKS** 1.4B ask questions/seek clarification/locate details about text **ELPS** 4D use prereading supports to comprehend texts; 4F use visual/contextual/peer/teacher support to read/comprehend texts

14

Meet the Author

Cynthia Rylant

As a young girl, Cynthia Rylant loved animals. She still does. Ms. Rylant lives with a dog and two cats. She puts animals in the books she writes, too.

Meet the Illustrator

Mark Teague

Mark Teague didn't go to art school. He taught himself to draw! He stays busy by working on more than one book at a time.

THE TREE

from POPPLETON FOREVER

by CYNTHIA RYLANT

illustrated by MARK TEAGUE

Poppleton planted a new little tree
in his yard.
It was a dogwood.
Poppleton liked it very much.

He watered it every day.

He gave it tree food.

He staked it against the wind.

The little tree grew strong and fast.

Poppleton was pleased.

Then one day the tree looked awful.

Its leaves drooped.

Its bark peeled.

It turned from green to brown.

"Oh no!" said Poppleton,

when he saw his tree.

He called the tree doctor.
"Come right away!" said Poppleton.
The tree doctor came to look at
Poppleton's tree.

✔ **STOP AND THINK**

Story Structure How
do you think Poppleton
will solve his problem?
Read to find out.

TEKS 1.4A; **ELPS** 4I

19

He tapped it. He stroked it.
He felt its trunk and leaves.
The tree doctor said to Poppleton,
"This tree needs something,
but I don't know what it is."

"Can't you just give it a pill?"
asked Poppleton.
"It isn't sick," said the tree doctor.
"It *needs* something."
Poppleton did not know
what his little tree needed.

He tapped it. He stroked it.
He felt its trunk and leaves.
But he did not know.
Poppleton sat up with his tree all
night, wondering what it needed.

In the morning he went for help.
"What does my tree need?" Poppleton
asked Hudson down the street.
"A piece of cheese?" said Hudson.
Poppleton gave the tree a piece
of cheese, but it didn't help.

"What does my tree need?" Poppleton
asked Newhouse, the delivery dog.
"A bone?" said Newhouse.

Poppleton gave the tree a
bone, but it didn't help.

Poppleton went to see Cherry Sue.
"What does my tree need?" Poppleton
asked Cherry Sue. Cherry Sue looked
out her window at the little tree.
She thought and thought.
Then she said, "If I were that tree,
I would need a bird feeder."

"A bird feeder?" asked Poppleton.
"Trees want birds," said Cherry
Sue. "Why do you think they hold
out their arms all day?"

Poppleton bought a bird feeder
for his little tree.

A sparrow came, and
a leaf turned green.

A cardinal came, and
another leaf turned green.

A bluebird came, and
three leaves turned green.

Poppleton's tree got better.
Soon all of its leaves were green.
"You are a pretty smart llama,"
Poppleton told Cherry Sue.
"You are a pretty nice pig," Cherry
Sue told him.
Then they had lemonade and watched
the birds.

1. In the story, the word <u>turned</u> means —

- ☐ tapped
- ☐ drove
- ☐ changed

TEKS 1.6C

2. 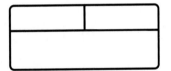 **Story Structure**

How does Cherry Sue solve Poppleton's problem? **TEKS** 1.4B, 1.9A, 1.9B, 1.24C, **ELPS** 4G

3. Oral Language Act out the story with four classmates. Use the Retelling Cards. **TEKS** 1.9A, RC–1(E)

Retelling Cards

 TEKS 1.4B ask questions/seek clarification/locate details about texts; 1.6C use syntax/context to determine meaning; 1.9A retell story events; 1.9B describe/analyze characters; 1.24C record information in visual formats; RC–1(E) retell/act out important story events; **ELPS** 4G demonstrate comprehension through shared reading/retelling/summarizing/responding/note-taking

I Read

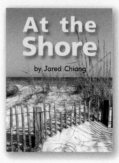

At the
Shore
by Jared Chiang

✔ **PHONICS SKILL**

Words with **ar**
Words with **or, ore**

✔ **WORDS TO KNOW**

pretty
window

TEKS **1.3A(i)** decode words with consonants; **1.3A(ii)** decode words with vowels; **1.3C(vi)** decode using r-controlled vowel pattern; **1.3H** identify/read high-frequency words; **ELPS** **4A** learn English sound-letter relationships/decode

At the Shore

by Jared Chiang

The shore is where land and sea meet. You can see sand, grass, and shells on the shore.

Carl's home is on the shore.
Carl can see the sea from
his window.

Mom, Carl, and Jill go for a short walk. Jill likes to see waves crash on the shore.

Tess is Carl's pal. She hunts
for pretty seashells.

Carl sees a crab in its shell. The crab will grow too big for that shell. Then it must find a shell that fits!

Carl and Tess see seagulls.
More and more seagulls will come.
Seagulls hunt for food in the sea
and on the shore.

Carl hopes he can get a sailboat. Carl will sail far. Then he will head back home at the shore.

Connect to Social Studies

GENRE

Informational text gives facts about a topic. Find facts about trees in this magazine article during shared reading.

TEXT FOCUS

A **bar graph** is a drawing that uses bars to compare numbers. Use the graph on p. 42 to find facts about trees.

It Comes from Trees

by Russ Andrew

You may never have thought about all the things that are made from trees! Trees can be turned into many useful things. They help make our lives better day and night.

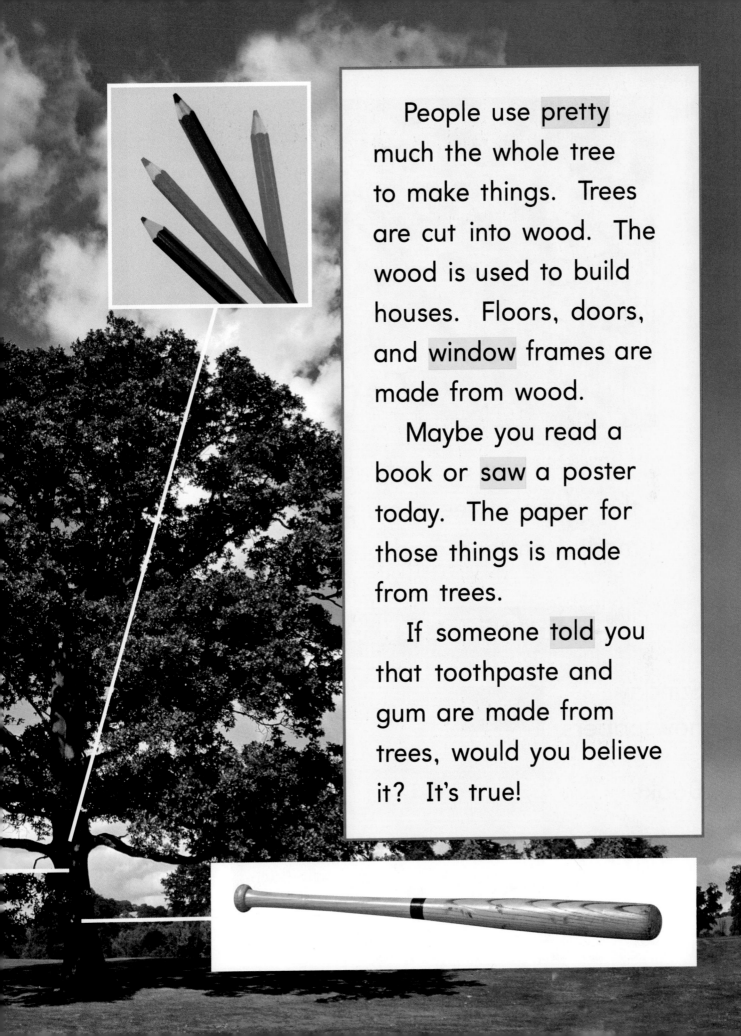

People use pretty much the whole tree to make things. Trees are cut into wood. The wood is used to build houses. Floors, doors, and window frames are made from wood.

Maybe you read a book or saw a poster today. The paper for those things is made from trees.

If someone told you that toothpaste and gum are made from trees, would you believe it? It's true!

This is one cord of wood. Look at the graph to see some paper products made from one cord of wood.

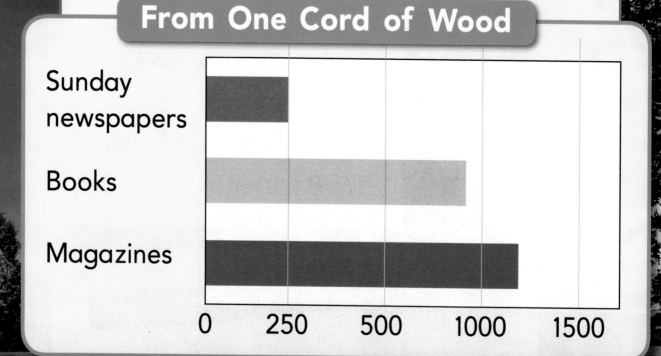

From One Cord of Wood

	0	250	500	1000	1500
Sunday newspapers					
Books					
Magazines					

Making Connections

Read Together

Text to Self

TEKS 1.7A, RC-1(F)

Connect to Experiences Think about how Poppleton cared for his tree. Write about something you have cared for.

Text to Text

TEKS 1.19C, RC-1(F)

List Ideas Why are the trees in both stories important? List your ideas.

Text to World

TEKS 1.27A, 1.28, 1.29, RC-1(F)

Think and Share Tell a partner how people help trees grow. Take turns listening. Speak clearly.

TEKS **1.7A** connect stories/fables to personal experiences; **1.19C** write brief comments on texts; **1.27A** listen attentively/ask relevant questions; **1.28** share information/ideas by speaking clearly; **1.29** follow discussion rules; **RC-1(F)** make connections to experiences/texts/community; **ELPS** **1G** distinguish between formal/informal English; **2I** demonstrate listening comprehension of spoken English; **3E** share information in cooperative learning interactions

Grammar

Subject Pronouns Words that can take the place of nouns are called **pronouns**. The pronouns **he**, **she**, and **it** name one. The pronouns **we** and **they** name more than one.

Ben watered the tree.
He watered the tree.

The tree grew.
It grew.

Birds loved the tree.
They loved the tree.

Lily fed the birds.
She fed the birds.

Choose the correct pronoun to name each picture. Write it on a sheet of paper. Then say a sentence to a partner about each picture. Use the pronoun.

1.   she   he

2.   they   it

3.   it   we

4.   they   she

5.   we   he

Grammar in Writing

When you proofread your writing, be sure you have used pronouns correctly.

Write to Express

Read
Together

✓ **Ideas**   Story **sentences** can tell the exact words characters say. These words help us understand how characters think and feel.

Niki wrote what Poppleton did next. Then she added words that told just what he said.

Revised Draft

Now Poppleton was hungry.
"I want some pizza," he said.
∧Cherry Sue was hungry, too.

Writing Traits Checklist

✓ **Ideas**   Did I write the exact words a character says?

✓ Do I need to add interesting details?

✓ Did I use pronouns correctly?

Look for the exact words Poppleton said in Niki's final copy. Then revise your own writing. Use the Checklist.

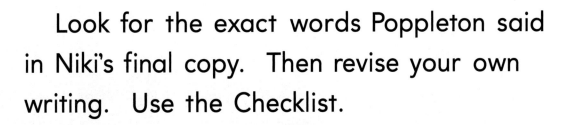

Final Copy

Snack Time

Now Poppleton was hungry.

"I want some pizza," he said.

Cherry Sue was hungry, too.

So they hopped on bikes and went to a pizza shop.

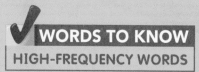

✓ **WORDS TO KNOW**
HIGH-FREQUENCY WORDS

learning

begins

until

eight

young

follow

years

baby

Vocabulary Reader

Context Cards

TEKS 1.3H identify/read high-frequency words; **ELPS** 1F use accessible language to learn new language; 3B expand/internalize initial English vocabulary

Words to Know

Read Together

- Read each Context Card.

- Make up a new sentence that uses a blue word.

1

learning

This baby giraffe is learning how to walk.

2

begins

The lion cub begins to get stronger.

3 until

These owls can't fly until they are older.

4 eight

The eight little swans go for a swim.

5 young

The young hippo will be very big soon.

6 follow

The bear cubs follow their mother.

7 years

An elephant can live for seventy years.

8 baby

This baby panda is eating plants.

Background  Read Together

✓ **WORDS TO KNOW** **Growing Up**

Many baby animals need help until they grow older. Young animals are learning as they follow their mothers around. A baby elephant may stay with its mother for many years. A kitten begins to care for itself before it is eight weeks old.

Animals and Their Babies

cat   kitten   bear   cub

elephant   calf   duck   duckling

50

TEKS 1.4C establish purpose/monitor comprehension; **1.14B** identify important facts/details; **RC-1(A)** establish reading purposes; **ELPS 1E** internalize new basic/academic language; **4F** use visual/contextual/peer/teacher support to read/comprehend texts

Comprehension  Read Together

 **TARGET SKILL** Conclusions

When you draw **conclusions**, you use details as clues to figure out things the author doesn't tell. Good readers find clues in the words and in the pictures. They also think about what they know from their own life.

> **Conclusion: The children are going to school. What clues helped you?**

As you read **Amazing Animals**, draw conclusions about why different animals have different body parts.

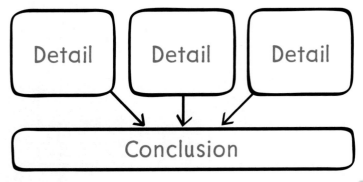

Detail   Detail   Detail

Conclusion

JOURNEYS DIGITAL Powered by
DESTINATIONReading®
Comprehension Activities: Lesson 22

51

Amazing Animals

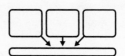

learning	young
begins	follow
until	years
eight	baby

✓ **TARGET SKILL**

Conclusions Use details to figure out more about a selection.

✓ **TARGET STRATEGY**

Visualize Picture what is happening as you read.

GENRE

Informational text gives facts about a topic.

TEKS **1.4B** ask questions/seek clarification/ locate details about texts; **1.11** recognize sensory details; **1.14B** identify important facts/ details; **RC-1(C)** monitor/adjust comprehension; **ELPS 4J** employ inferential skills to demonstrate comprehension

Meet the Author

Gwendolyn Hooks

Gwendolyn Hooks wrote this story because she loves animals. "This story is about wild animals," she explains.

"I don't own any wild animals, but I do have a pet cat."

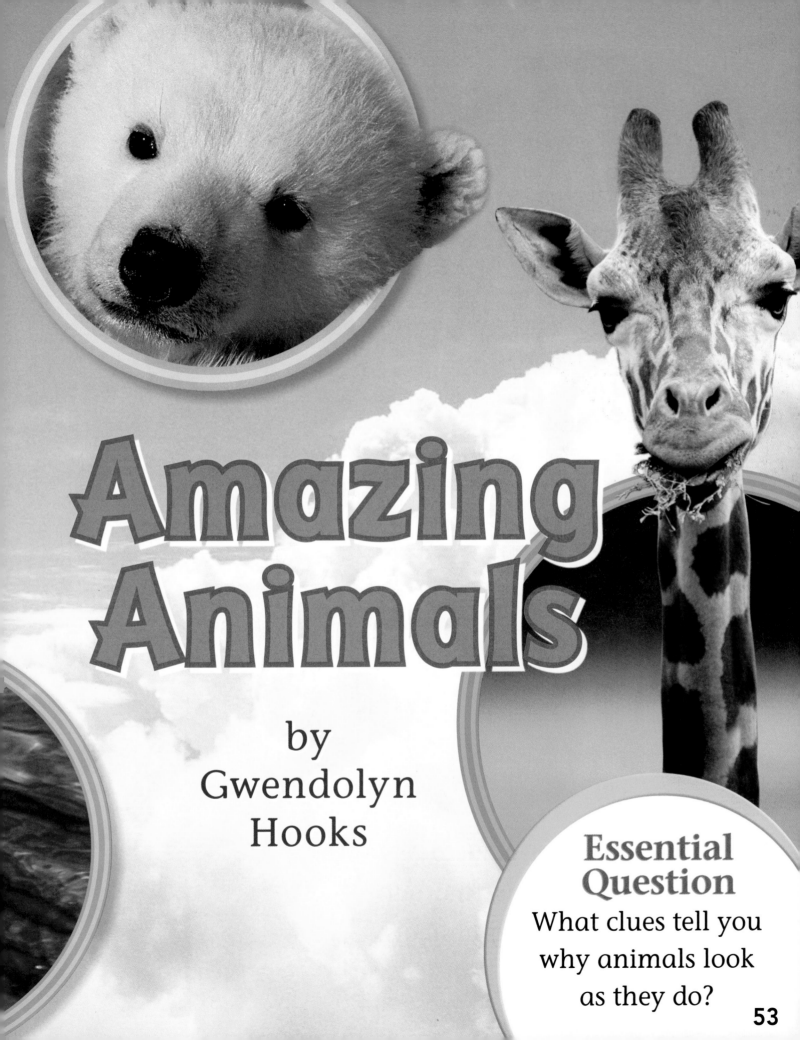

Amazing Animals

by
Gwendolyn
Hooks

Essential Question

What clues tell you why animals look as they do?

53

Big eyes,

long beak,

thick fur,

big squeak!

Animals get a lot of help as they grow up. Let's find out about eight amazing animals.

Polar Bear

A polar bear has thick fur. Each hair is like a tube. The hair has no color, like glass. The sun makes it look white.

How does thick, white fur help?

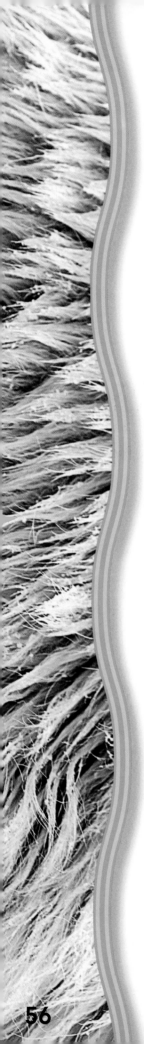

Thick fur helps polar bears stay warm. The color of their fur looks the same as snow. This helps them hide.

Where does this cute young polar bear like to hide?

Elephant

An elephant has a long nose. The nose is called a trunk. It takes many years for an elephant to grow two big teeth. These teeth are called tusks.

How do tusks and a trunk help?

Elephants use their tusks to scrape
bark off trees. Then they eat the
bark. These elephants are learning
to use their trunks to get water.

Sometimes they will spray water at
a friend!

Camel

Some camels have one hump. Some have two. All camels have two rows of eyelashes.

How do humps and thick eyelashes help?

59

A camel's hump has fat inside. On long trips, a camel's body uses the fat for food. A camel's eyelashes keep out the desert sand.

This baby camel will follow his mother when the herd goes from place to place.

Duck

A duck is a bird. It has two feet, and each foot has three toes. A duck has a beak, too.

How do feet and a beak help?

Ducks use their feet to swim in the water or walk on land. They use their beaks to eat plants and bugs.

Look! This duck uses her beak to clean her friend.

Giraffe

A giraffe has spots. A giraffe
has a long neck.

How do spots and a long
neck help?

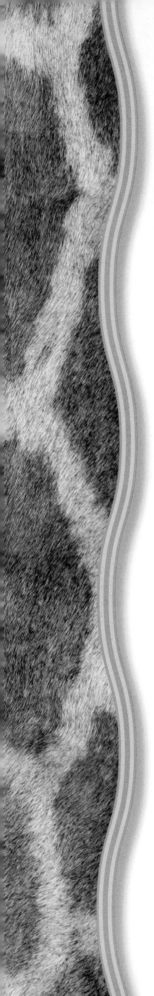

A giraffe's spots help it hide. A giraffe's long neck helps it reach the leaves of trees.

This giraffe's long neck helps her reach her baby. She gives him a big kiss!

Porcupine

A porcupine has soft quills when it is born. The quills get sharp in a day or two.

How do quills help?

Quills help keep a porcupine safe. If an animal begins to come too close, the porcupine backs into it. The sharp quills hurt!

Quills tell this cub to stay away!

✔️ **STOP AND THINK**

Conclusions

Why would a porcupine want animals to stay away?

TEKS RC-1(D), ELPS 4J

Turtle

A turtle has a shell that is very hard.

How does a hard shell help?

67

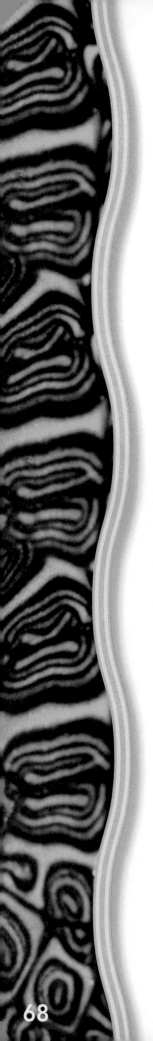

A turtle can hide inside its shell from an animal that may hurt it. The turtle waits until the animal goes away. Then the turtle comes back out.

You're safe now, turtle!

Dolphin

A dolphin's tail has two parts called flukes. A dolphin has two flippers.

How do tail flukes and flippers help?

A dolphin flips its tail flukes up and down to swim fast. It uses its flippers to turn to the left or right.

These two dolphins swim away fast. Who will be first?

Have fun, dolphins!

Read Together

Your Turn

1. In the selection, the word <u>begins</u> means —

- ⬭ starts
- ⬭ finishes
- ⬭ begs

TEKS 1.6C

2. ✔ **TARGET SKILL** **Conclusions** Why does a porcupine have quills? **TEKS** 1.4B, 1.14B, 1.24C

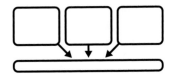

3. Oral Language Tell a partner how each animal's special body parts help that animal. Speak clearly. **TEKS** 1.14B, 1.14C, 1.28, **ELPS** 4G

 TEKS **1.4B** ask questions/seek clarification/locate details about texts; **1.6C** use syntax/context to determine meaning; **1.14B** identify important facts/details; **1.14C** retell order of events; **1.24C** record information in visual formats; **1.28** share information/ideas by speaking clearly; **ELPS** **4G** demonstrate comprehension through shared reading/retelling/responding/note-taking

Fox and Crow

retold by Melissa Rothman
illustrated by Tom Sperling

✔ **PHONICS SKILL**

Words with **er, ir, ur**

✔ **WORDS TO KNOW**

learning
years

TEKS **1.3A(i)** decode words with consonants; **1.3A(ii)** decode words with vowels; **1.3C(vi)** decode using r-controlled vowel pattern; **1.3H** identify/read high-frequency words; **ELPS 4A** learn English sound-letter relationships/decode

Fox and Crow

retold by Melissa Rothman
illustrated by Tom Sperling

Crow is perched in a birch tree.
She sees some grapes. She grabs the
grapes and goes back to her perch.

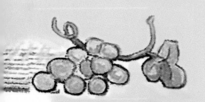

73

Fox passes by. It seems as if he has not had a meal in years.

Fox thinks, "If that bird speaks, she will drop those grapes."

First Fox asks, "What is
your name?"
Crow turns her back.

Next Fox asks, "Crow, are you feeling well?"

Crow will not speak. Crow will not stir.

Then Fox tells Crow, "It's sad that
a bird as nice as you cannot sing."
Crow whirls, and then she blurts,
"Sir, I am learning to sing!"

The grapes land in soft dirt. As Crow sings, Fox eats them up. Then he smiles, turns, and trots off.

Fox tricked Crow this time, but Crow has learned. Fox will not trick her next time!

The
Ugly
Duckling

Connect to Traditional Tales

✔ **WORDS TO KNOW**

learning	young
begins	follow
until	years
eight	baby

GENRE

A **fairy tale** is an old story with characters that can do amazing things.

TEXT FOCUS

Many fairy tales begin **Once upon a time** and end **happily ever after.** What do these words mean in this story?

TEKS **1.3H** identify/read high-frequency words; **1.7B** understand recurring phrases in traditional tales; **ELPS 4I** employ reading skills to demonstrate comprehension

The Ugly Duckling

Once upon a time, a duck sat on eight eggs. One day, all but one of the eggs hatched. The ducks waited until the last baby bird came out. He was big and gray. The other ducks thought he was ugly.

Each day the ducklings would follow Mother Duck. They were learning to be ducks. The other ducks did not want to play with the ugly duckling. He felt sad. One day he left.

Winter soon came. A farmer found the ugly duckling. "I must take you home before it begins to snow," he said.

When spring came, the farmer took the duckling to a pond. The duckling saw himself in the water. He felt like many years had passed. He had changed!

Now he knew he was not an ugly duckling. He was a young swan. He and the other swans lived happily ever after.

Making Connections

Read Together

 Text to Self

TEKS 1.19A, RC-1(F)

Write Sentences Draw your favorite animal. Write sentences to tell your classmates about it.

 Text to Text

TEKS 1.10, 1.28, RC-1(F)

Compare Selections Which selection is true? Which selection is make-believe? What questions do you have about the selections? Talk about the selections with three classmates. Speak clearly.

 Text to World

TEKS 1.29, RC-1(F)

Connect to Science What is the same about how baby animals and baby children grow? What is different? Tell your ideas. Take turns with a partner.

 TEKS **1.10** distinguish true stories from fantasies; **1.19A** write brief compositions; **1.28** share information/ideas by speaking clearly; **1.29** follow discussion rules; **RC-1(F)** make connections to experiences/texts/community; **ELPS 2I** demonstrate listening comprehension of spoken English; **3E** share information in cooperative learning interactions; **5B** write using new basic/content-based vocabulary

TEKS 1.20A(vi) understand/use pronouns; 1.21B(ii) capitalize pronoun "I"; ELPS 1G distinguish between formal/informal English; 5E employ increasingly complex grammatical structures in writing

Grammar

The Pronoun I Always use the **pronoun I** in the subject of a sentence. Name yourself last when you talk about yourself and another person.

Correct

Sara and I like baby animals.

Not Correct

I and Sara like baby animals.
Sara and me like baby animals.
Me and Sara like baby animals.

Write the correct words to finish each sentence. Use another sheet of paper. Read your sentences to a partner.

1. _____?_____ watched a piglet.
   Dad and I   I and Dad

2. _____?_____ saw baby cubs.
   Me and Liz   Liz and I

3. _____?_____ petted the foal.
   Tom and me   Tom and I

4. _____?_____ fed one kitten.
   I and Ana   Ana and I

5. _____?_____ heard chicks.
   Jake and I   Me and Jake

Grammar in Writing

When you proofread your writing, be sure you have used the pronoun **I** correctly. Remember to capitalize the prounoun **I**.

TEKS **1.6A** identify nouns/verbs; **1.17C** revise drafts; **1.17D** edit drafts; **1.20A(i)** understand/use verbs; **1.20A(vii)** understand/use time-order transition words; **ELPS** **5D** edit writing for standard grammar/usage; **5E** employ increasingly complex grammatical structures in writing; **5G** narrate/describe/explain in writing

Write to Express

Read Together

✔ **Word Choice** Good story **sentences** have exact verbs that help readers picture what the story characters are doing.

Troy wrote about a baby bird. Later, he changed **went** to a more exact verb.

Revised Draft

Then Jay ~~went~~ flew into the air.

Writing Traits Checklist

✔ **Word Choice** Do my sentences have exact verbs?

✔ Did I tell what happened in order?

✔ Do I need to delete any words that do not belong?

86

Identify words that name actions in Troy's final copy. Then revise your writing to include exact verbs. Use the Checklist.

Final Copy

Flying Lesson

Jay stood quietly by the nest.

First, he watched his mom.

Then Jay flew into the air.

He sailed high above the garden.

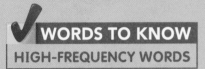
✓ WORDS TO KNOW
HIGH-FREQUENCY WORDS

house

along

together

boy

father

again

nothing

began

Vocabulary Reader	Context Cards

TEKS **1.3H** identify/read high-frequency words; **ELPS** **1F** use accessible language to learn new language; **3B** expand/internalize initial English vocabulary

Words to Know

Read Together

- Read each Context Card.
- Ask a question that uses one of the blue words.

1
house
They learned how to build a house for birds.

2
along
He rode carefully along the bike path.

3 together

The baby can clap her hands **together** now.

4 boy

The **boy** teaches his sister to read.

5 father

My **father** teaches me how to swim.

6 again

We went out on the ice **again** to practice.

7 nothing

At first **nothing** fit, but he finished the puzzle.

8 began

She **began** to take violin lessons.

Background

Read Together

✓ WORDS TO KNOW **Puppy Training**

A boy and his father were teaching their puppy to walk on a leash. They walked together along a path. Suddenly the leash dropped, and the puppy began to run. Nothing could stop her. The boy whistled again and again. At last, the puppy came to him. They all walked back to the house.

- **What pets do you like?**
- **What would you teach a pet to do?**

TEKS 1.4C establish purpose/monitor comprehension; **RC-1(A)** establish reading purposes; **ELPS** 1E internalize new basic/academic language; 4F use visual/contextual/peer/teacher support to read/comprehend texts

Comprehension

✔ **TARGET SKILL**   Cause and Effect

Sometimes one story event causes another event to happen. The **cause** happens first. It is the reason why something else happens. The **effect** is what happens next. Good readers think about:

What happened?
Why did it happen?

Cause: The light turned red. What is the **effect**?

As you read **Whistle for Willie**, think about what happens when Peter tries to whistle.

What happens?	Why?

JOURNEYS DIGITAL Powered by DESTINATIONReading·
Comprehension Activities: Lesson 23

✔ **TARGET SKILL**

Cause and Effect Tell what happens and why.

✔ **TARGET STRATEGY**

Monitor/Clarify Find ways to figure out what doesn't make sense.

GENRE

Realistic fiction is a story that could happen in real life.

TEKS **1.4B** ask questions/seek clarification/ locate details about texts; **1.4C** establish purpose/monitor comprehension; **RC-1C** monitor/adjust comprehension **ELPS** **4D** use prereading supports to comprehend texts

Meet the Author and Illustrator

Ezra Jack Keats

Ezra Jack Keats writes and illustrates books for children. When Mr. Keats was a boy, he drew pictures on the kitchen table. His mother was so proud, she kept the art rather than wash the table.

WHISTLE FOR WILLIE

by Ezra Jack Keats

Essential Question

What causes events in a story to happen?

93

Oh, how Peter wished he could whistle!

He saw a boy playing with his dog. Whenever the boy whistled, the dog ran straight to him.

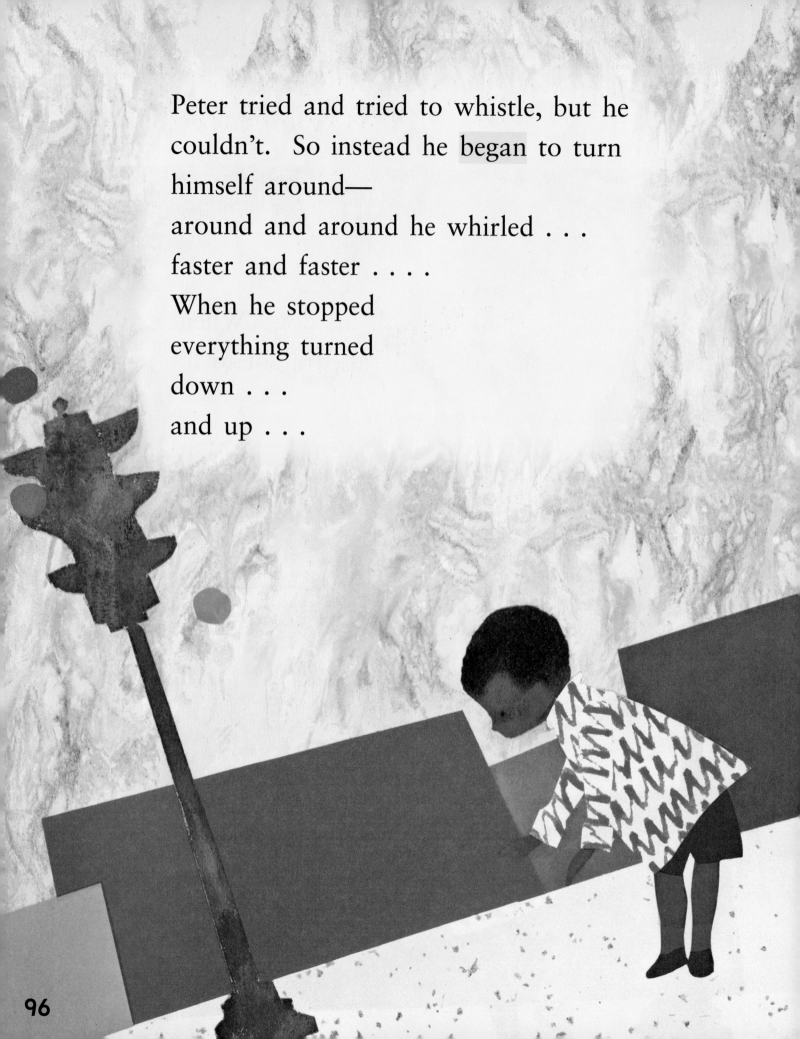

Peter tried and tried to whistle, but he couldn't. So instead he began to turn himself around—
around and around he whirled . . .
faster and faster . . . .
When he stopped
everything turned
down . . .
and up . . .

and up . . .
and down . . .
and around
and around.

Peter saw his dog, Willie, coming.
Quick as a wink, he hid in an empty
carton lying on the sidewalk.

"Wouldn't it be funny if I whistled?" Peter thought. "Willie would stop and look all around to see who it was."

Peter tried again to whistle—but still he couldn't. So Willie just walked on.

> ✔ **STOP AND THINK**
> **Cause and Effect** What do you think will happen if Peter tries to whistle again? Read to find out.
> **TEKS** 1.4A; **ELPS** 4I

Peter got out of the carton and started home.
On the way he took some colored chalks out
of his pocket and drew a long, long line
right up to his door.

He stood there and tried to whistle
again. He blew till his cheeks were
tired. But nothing happened.

He went into his house and put on his father's old hat to make himself feel more grown-up. He looked into the mirror to practice whistling. Still no whistle!

When his mother saw what he was doing,
Peter pretended that he was his father.
He said, "I've come home early today, dear.
Is Peter here?"
His mother answered, "Why no, he's outside
with Willie."
"Well, I'll go out and look for them," said Peter.

First he walked along a crack in the sidewalk. Then he tried to run away from his shadow.

He jumped off his shadow. But when he landed they were together again.

He came to the corner
where the carton was,
and who should he see
but Willie!

Peter scrambled under the carton.
He blew and blew.
Suddenly—out came a real whistle!

Willie stopped and looked around to
see who it was.

"It's me," Peter shouted, and stood up.
Willie raced straight to him.

110

Peter ran home to show his father and
mother what he could do.
They loved Peter's whistling. So did Willie.

Peter's mother asked him and Willie
to go on an errand to the grocery store.
He whistled all the way there,
and he whistled all the way home.

Read Together

YourTurn

---

1. In the story, the word <u>again</u> means —

⬭ once more

⬭ not ever

⬭ long ago

TEKS 1.3H, 1.6C

---

2. 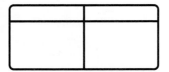 **TARGET SKILL** **Cause and Effect**

What happens when Peter sees the boy whistle for his dog? **TEKS** 1.9B, 1.24C

3. Oral Language How would Willie tell the story? Use a stick puppet of Willie to tell the story. **TEKS** 1.9A, 1.14C, RC–1(D); **ELPS** 4G

 TEKS **1.3H** identify/read high-frequency words; **1.6C** use syntax/context to determine meaning; **1.9A** retell story events; **1.9B** describe/analyze characters; **1.14C** retell order of events; **1.24C** record information in visual formats; **RC–1(D)** make inferences/use textual evidence; **ELPS** **4G** demonstrate comprehension through shared reading/retelling/responding/note-taking

Good Homes
by Louise Tidd

Good Homes

by Louise Tidd

These insects are bees. Bees
live together in hives. Hives are
good homes for bees.

Each hive has a queen. The queen bee does nothing but lay eggs. That is her job. These bees feed their queen bee.

Caves make good homes for bats. Bats sleep all day. They hook their back feet in cracks. Bats sleep upside down.

It is dark when bats wake up. Bats
hear much better than they can see.
Bats make squeaks to tell if it is safe.

This cute fellow is a rabbit. Rabbits
dig burrows. A burrow is a big hole.

If one rabbit sees a problem, it thumps its foot. Then the rabbits run back in their burrow to be safe.

Hives, caves, and burrows make good animal homes. This is not an animal home. It is for kids. Can you tell what it is?

Connect to Poetry

house	father
along	again
together	nothing
boy	began

GENRE

Poetry uses words to show pictures and feelings. Listen for interesting words in each poem. Clap along with the rhythm, or beat.

TEXT FOCUS

Rhyme is words with the same ending sound. Which poems use rhyme?

 TEKS **1.3H** identify/read high-frequency words; **1.8** respond to/use rhythm/rhyme/alliteration; **ELPS** **4G** demonstrate comprehension through shared reading/retelling/responding/note-taking

Pet Poems

This poem began as a folk song. Read it along with your class. Then sing it together.

Bingo

There was a farmer had a dog,
And Bingo was his name, O!
B – I – N – G – O,
B – I – N – G – O,
B – I – N – G – O,

And Bingo was his name, O!

Can someone in your class read this poem in Spanish? Now read it again in English.

Caballito blanco, reblanco

Caballito blanco,
reblanco,
sácame de aquí,
llévame hasta el puerto
donde yo nací.

Little White Horse

Little horse
White as snow
Take me where
I long to go.
Take me to the port
By the sea
Where I was born
And long to be.

traditional folk poem

What kind of pet would you like in your house? Your mother or father can help you decide.

PET SNAKE

No trace of fuzz.
No bit of fur.
No growling bark,
or gentle purr.
No cozy cuddle.
No sloppy kiss.
All he really does
is hisssssssssss.

by Rebecca Kai Dotlich

Write About a Pet

Write a poem about a pet. Use words with the same beginning sounds. Try to use the words boy and nothing, too.

Making Connections

Read Together

 Text to Self   TEKS 1.28, 1.29, RC-1(F)

Talk About Pets Tell a partner about a pet you would like to have. Take turns and speak clearly.

 Text to Text   TEKS 1.4B, 1.19C, RC-1(F)

Make a Poster How is Willie different from the pet snake in the poem? Draw Willie. Write words that tell what he looks like and what he can do.

 Text to World   TEKS RC-1(F)

Connect to Math Make a list of pets. Count how many classmates like each kind of pet.

 TEKS **1.4B** ask questions/seek clarification/locate details about texts; **1.19C** write brief comments on texts; **1.28** share information/ideas by speaking clearly; **1.29** follow discussion rules; **RC-1(F)** make connections to experiences/texts/community; **ELPS 1E** internalize new basic/academic language; **2I** demonstrate listening comprehension of spoken English; **5B** write using new basic/content-based vocabulary

Grammar

Possessive Pronouns Some **pronouns** show that something belongs to someone. This kind of pronoun can come before a noun or at the end of a sentence.

This is **my** dog. This dog is **mine**.
I am using **your** chalk. The chalk is **yours**.
That is **his** shadow. That shadow is **his**.
I am wearing **her** hat. This hat is **hers**.

Write the correct pronoun
to finish each sentence.
Use another sheet of paper.

1. I have a dog. Little Cleo is _____**?**_____ .

    mine   mines

2. This is her dish. The dish is _____**?**_____ .

    his   hers

3. I whistle. Cleo hears _____**?**_____ whistle.

    my   mine

4. She follows me to _____**?**_____ house.

    your   they

5. Cleo loves the fish that are _____**?**_____ !

    your   yours

Grammar in Writing

When you proofread your writing, be sure
you have used pronouns correctly.

TEKS 1.17C revise drafts; 1.17D edit drafts; **ELPS** 5D edit writing for standard grammar/usage; 5E employ increasingly complex grammatical structures in writing

Write to Express

✓ Organization When you write sentences for a story **summary**, tell the important events in the order they happened.

Abby wrote a summary of part of **Whistle for Willie**. Later, she moved one sentence.

Revised Draft

Peter kept trying to whistle.

He practiced in a mirror.

He went into his house.

Writing Traits Checklist

✓ Organization Did I tell the events in order?

✓ Do I need to add more important details?

✓ Did I use the correct pronouns?

128

Look for events in the correct order in Abby's final copy. Then write and revise your own draft. Put your ideas in order as you write your sentences. Use the Checklist.

Final Copy

Whistle for Willie

Peter kept trying to whistle.

Then he went into his house.

He practiced in a mirror.

When his mom saw him, he pretended to be his dad.

✓ **WORDS TO KNOW**
HIGH-FREQUENCY WORDS

ready

anything

upon

kind

places

also

flower

warm

Vocabulary
Reader

Context
Cards

TEKS 1.3H identify/read high-frequency
words; **ELPS** 3B expand/internalize initial
English vocabulary

Words to Know

Read Together

- Read each Context Card.
- Describe a picture, using the blue word.

1
ready
This butterfly is getting ready to fly.

2
anything
Do you know anything about butterflies?

3 upon

A butterfly rests upon the leaf.

4 kind

There is more than one kind of butterfly.

5 places

Butterflies land on this tree in many places.

6 also

Butterflies are insects. Ants are also insects.

7 flower

This butterfly drinks from the flower.

8 warm

Butterflies like the warm sun.

Background

Read Together

✓ WORDS TO KNOW **A Caterpillar's Story**

I grew in an egg, and now I crawl. I do not eat anything but a special kind of leaf. I'm eating a lot and also growing quickly. When I am ready, I will change. Then I'll be able to fly to warm places. I'll find a pretty flower to sit upon. What do you learn about me from my picture?

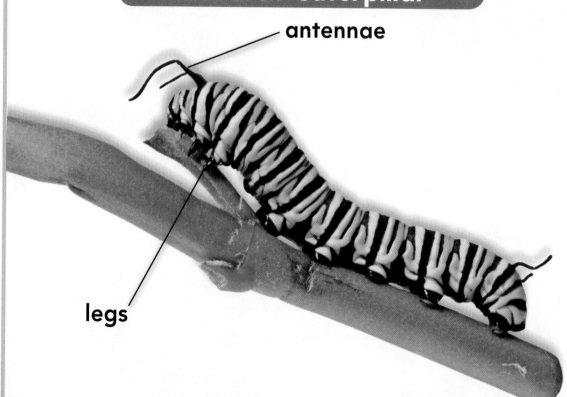

Monarch Caterpillar

antennae

legs

TEKS 1.4C establish purpose/monitor comprehension; **1.14C** retell order of events; **1.24C** record information in visual formats; **RC-1(A)** establish reading purposes; **ELPS 1E** internalize new basic/academic language; **4F** use visual/contextual/peer/teacher support to read/comprehend texts

Comprehension  Read Together

✓ **TARGET SKILL**   Sequence of Events

Many selections tell about things in the order in which they happen. This order is called the **sequence of events**. Think about what happens first, next, and last as you read.

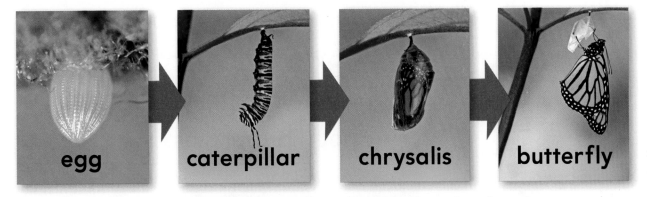

egg → caterpillar → chrysalis → butterfly

As you read **A Butterfly Grows**, think about how a caterpillar becomes a butterfly. Use a chart to keep track of the sequence of events. Then use the chart and the words in the selection to retell the events in order.

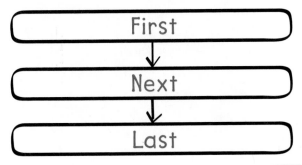

First
↓
Next
↓
Last

JOURNEYS DIGITAL   **Powered by** DESTINATION Reading
Comprehension Activities: Lesson 24

133

ready   places
anything   also
upon   flower
kind   warm

Sequence of Events
Tell the order in which
things happen.

Question Ask questions
about what you read.

GENRE
Narrative nonfiction
gives facts but has
make-believe parts.

TEKS **1.4B** ask questions/seek clarification/
locate details about texts; **1.9A** retell story
events; **1.14C** retell order of events; **1.27A**
listen attentively/ask questions; **RC-1(B)** ask literal
questions; **RC-1(E)** retell/act out important story events

Meet the Author

Steve Swinburne

Steve Swinburne loves
nature—especially butterflies!
He planted a garden at his
house filled with flowers that
butterflies like. He took many
of the pictures for **A Butterfly
Grows** in his garden. He
hopes you enjoy learning
about butterflies.

A Butterfly Grows

by Stephen Swinburne

Essential Question

Why do authors put events in a certain order?

135

Can you see me
on the plant?

I am a little caterpillar!
I grew in an egg. When I
was ready, I hatched!

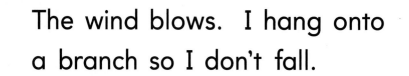
The wind blows. I hang onto
a branch so I don't fall.

Rain falls. It plips and plops.
I need to drink water to live,
so I drink the small drops.

This milkweed plant is my food.
I need food so I can grow.

I eat this leaf for lunch.
Chew, chew!
Crunch, munch!

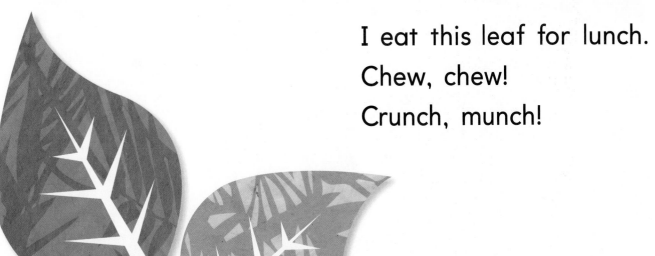

I eat and grow,
eat and grow.

Look how big I grew!
My skin is so snug.

142

I look for a spot to rest.
Soon I will shed my skin.

At last I am a chrysalis. I'm
an inch long. Then, in ten days,
I am ready to come out.

 STOP AND THINK

Sequence of Events
What will the caterpillar look like after
it comes out? Read on to find out.

TEKS 1.4A, ELPS 4J

Look at me now!
Do you see anything new?

145

I am an insect now.
I have six legs and
large wings.

My wings help me fly. Watch me fly!
I have fun! My wings also help me
go find plants for food.

I like to fly with all my friends.
We fly to warm places in the fall.
We eat food along the way.

148

I land upon a flower. Watch me
eat now! I sip and sip. Do you
know what kind of insect I am?

I am a butterfly!
I'm a beautiful butterfly!

150

1. In the story, the word <u>kind</u> means —

○ nice

○ type

○ warm

TEKS 1.3H, 1.6C

2. 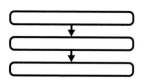 **Sequence of Events**

Think about what happens after the caterpillar finds a spot to rest. Retell the order of events by using the pictures in the story. **TEKS** 1.14B, 1.14C, 1.24C

3. Oral Language With a partner, take turns telling how a butterfly grows. Tell the events in order. Use the Retelling Cards. **TEKS** 1.14C, **ELPS** 4G

Retelling Cards

 TEKS 1.3H identify/read high-frequency words; **1.6C** use syntax/context to determine meaning; **1.14B** identify important facts/details; **1.14C** retell order of events; **1.24C** record information in visual formats; **ELPS 4G** demonstrate comprehension through shared reading/retelling/responding/note-taking

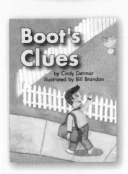
Boot's Clues

by Cindy Detmar
illustrated by Bill Brandon

Drew had to take a trip. He left Boot with Sue.

"Thanks," Drew said. "Boot's clues will tell you what to do."

Boot ran and ran. He picked
up a stick and gave it to Sue.
"Is this a clue?" asked Sue.
"What kind of clue is this, Boot?"
Boot gave Sue a grin.

Sue threw the stick. Boot jumped up.

"He got it! It's a clue!" yelled Sue.

Sue and Boot went inside.
Boot bumped his food bowl
with his nose.

"Is this a clue?" asked Sue.

"That is a neat clue, Boot!"
said Sue. "You let me know
that you need food and water."

Then Sue gave a clue. She
turned off the light to see if Boot
would hop upon his bed. Did
he do it?

"You did it, Boot!" said Sue.
"You are cute! You give clues
and you get clues."

Connect to Science

✔ **WORDS TO KNOW**

ready	places
anything	also
upon	flower
kind	warm

GENRE

Readers' theater is text that has been written for people to read aloud.

TEXT FOCUS

Dialogue is the speaking parts in a play. You learn about characters from what they say. After reading, describe the characters.

 **TEKS** **1.3E** read words with inflectional endings; **1.3H** identify/read high-frequency words; **1.9B** describe/analyze characters

Readers' Theater

Best Friends

by Stephen Gill

Cast

Butterfly

Bird

Butterfly: Hi! What kind of butterfly are you?

Bird: I'm not a butterfly, silly. Can you think of anything else I could be?

Butterfly: Give me some clues!

Bird: Okay. I grow in an egg, and then I hatch.

Me, too!

 I have wings to help me fly.

 Me, too!

 I eat seeds and insects.

 Oh, no! I am an insect. Will you eat me?

 No! Birds like me eat many insects, but not butterflies.

 You just said you are a bird!

Oops, silly me! You know what I am!

 Are you ready to find a snack? I'll
land upon a flower and sip and sip.
You can find an insect on a leaf.

 We can also fly together. Then we'll
find warm places to rest.

 What a nice day for two best friends!

Making Connections

 Read Together

 Text to Self

Write a Response Write about a day you spend with the butterfly in **A Butterfly Grows**. Tell what you do.

 Text to Text

Connect to Science What facts did you learn from the selections? Which parts of these selections are make-believe? How do you know?

Text to World

Describe a Friend Draw a picture of you and your best friend having fun together. Tell a partner reasons why your best friend is your favorite.

 TEKS 1.10 distinguish true stories from fantasies; **1.19C** write brief comments on texts; **1.28** share information/ideas by speaking clearly; **RC-1(F)** make connections to experiences/texts/community; **ELPS 1E** internalize new basic/academic language; **5B** write using new basic/content-based vocabulary

163

TEKS 1.20A(i) understand/use verbs; 1.20A(vi) understand/use pronouns; ELPS 1G distinguish between formal/informal English; 5D edit writing for standard grammar/usage; 5E employ increasingly complex grammatical structures in writing

Grammar

Pronouns and Verbs Add **s** to most **verbs** when they tell about a **pronoun** that names one.

One	More Than One
It eat<u>s</u>. He grow<u>s</u>.	They eat. We grow.

Use **am** with the pronoun **I**. Use **is** with other pronouns that name one. Use **are** with pronouns that name more than one.

One	More Than One
I am hungry. She is full.	We are hungry. They are full.

Write the correct verb to finish each sentence. Use another sheet of paper. Take turns reading the sentences with a partner.

1. I _____**?**_____ with my uncle.
   am   is

2. We _____**?**_____ in a park.
   is   are

3. He _____**?**_____ two butterflies.
   see   sees

4. They _____**?**_____ on a flower.
   land   lands

5. The flower _____**?**_____ pink.
   is   are

Grammar in Writing

When you proofread your writing, be sure you have written the correct verb to go with each pronoun.

Reading-Writing Workshop: Prewrite

Write to Express (Read Together)

✓ Ideas When you plan a **story**, think about your characters. How do they look? What do they like? What problem do they have?

Deval drew pictures of his characters. Then he wrote clear details about them.

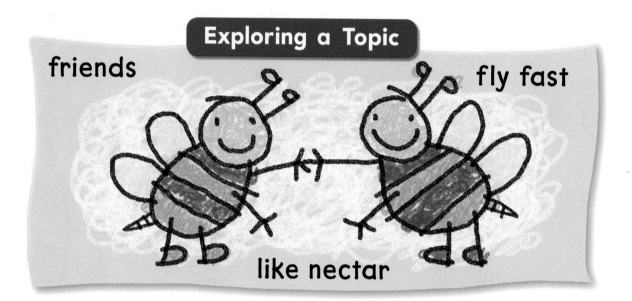

Exploring a Topic

friends

fly fast

like nectar

Prewriting Checklist

✓ Did I write details to describe my characters?

✓ Did I plan a problem my characters will solve?

✓ Does my story idea have a beginning, a middle, and an end?

166

Look for a problem Deval's characters will solve in his Story Map. Now make a Story Map for your own story. Use the Checklist.

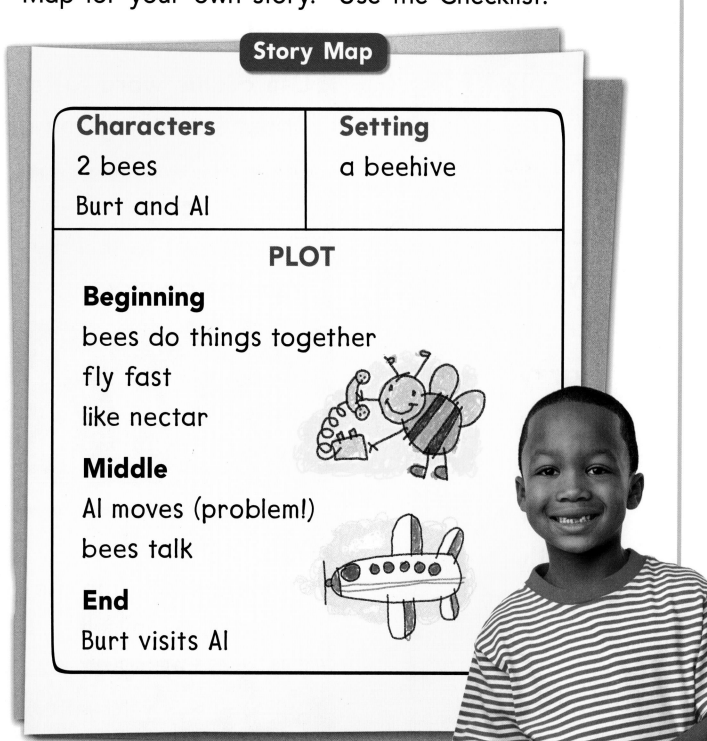

Story Map

Characters	Setting
2 bees Burt and Al	a beehive

PLOT

Beginning

bees do things together

fly fast

like nectar

Middle

Al moves (problem!)

bees talk

End

Burt visits Al

  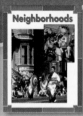

✓ **WORDS TO KNOW**
HIGH-FREQUENCY WORDS

city

myself

school

party

seven

buy

please

family

Vocabulary
Reader

Context
Cards

 TEKS **1.3H** identify/read high-frequency words; **ELPS** **1F** use accessible language to learn new language; **3B** expand/internalize initial English vocabulary

Words to Know

Read Together

● Read each Context Card.

● Use a blue word to tell about something you did.

1
city
They moved to the city from the country.

2
myself
I took the box into the house all by myself.

3 school

He met many new friends at school.

4 party

They had a party for their new classmate.

5 seven

She will bring seven apples to school.

6 buy

She will buy a plant for her friend.

7 please

"Please play with us," they said.

8 family

They invited the family to come in.

Background

✓ WORDS TO KNOW Moving Away

What might happen if your family moved to a new city? You might need seven boxes to pack your things. You might ask, "Can I pack these myself, please?" At your old school, friends might have a party for you and buy you a gift!

What would you pack if you were moving? What would remind you of your old friends?

TEKS 1.4C establish purpose/monitor comprehension; **1.9B** describe/analyze characters; **RC-1(A)** establish reading purposes; **ELPS** 1E internalize new basic/academic language; **4F** use visual/contextual/peer/teacher support to read/comprehend texts

Comprehension

Read Together

 **TARGET SKILL** Understanding Characters

Remember that you can learn a lot about story **characters** from the things they say and do. Use what characters say and do as clues to figure out how they feel and why they act as they do.

Characters: boy, girl, king, queen
What other characters could be in this story?

As you read **The New Friend**, find out about the new friend and what the boys say, do, and feel.

Speaking	Acting	Feeling

JOURNEYS DIGITAL
Powered by DESTINATIONReading®
Comprehension Activities: Lesson 25

The New Friend

city	seven
myself	buy
school	please
party	family

✔ **TARGET SKILL**

Understanding Characters Tell more about characters.

✔ **TARGET STRATEGY**

Summarize Stop to tell important events as you read.

GENRE

Realistic fiction is a story that could happen in real life.

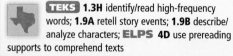 **TEKS** **1.3H** identify/read high-frequency words; **1.9A** retell story events; **1.9B** describe/analyze characters; **ELPS** **4D** use prereading supports to comprehend texts

Meet the Author

María Puncel

María Puncel lives in Spain. She writes her books in Spanish. Many of them have been translated into English, including **El Amigo Nuevo**.

Meet the Illustrator

Ed Martinez

Ed Martinez grew up with a painter in the family. His father was an artist! As a boy, Mr. Martinez got started by drawing horses. Now he draws pictures for magazines and books.

The New Friend

by María Puncel • illustrations by Ed Martinez

Essential Question

What clues tell you what a character is like?

173

Martin, Luis, and I lived in the city. Next door was an old house. No one had lived there for a long time.

One day a work crew came with pails and brushes. They started to wash and paint the empty house.

After they were done, and the paint had dried, the house looked pretty and new.

The next day a big truck pulled up. It was full of crates and boxes. A crew unloaded the boxes off the truck. A new family would soon live there.

Today Luis went over to the house next door. He met a boy called Makoto. Then we all met Makoto. Makoto was seven years old—just like us.

Before long, we found out that Makoto played soccer. He could keep running and running. He was good at learning things, too. He learned all of our names by the end of the game.

Soon Makoto's family was all moved in. We met his mother and father. They were glad that Makoto had made some new friends.

✔ STOP AND THINK

Understanding Characters

Why are Makoto's parents glad Makoto made new friends?

TEKS 1.9B, RC-1(D), **ELPS** 4J

While Makoto's mother and father went to buy food, Makoto stayed and played with us.

When Makoto's mother and father rejoined us, Martin, Makoto, and I helped them carry the bags into the house.

Makoto said he would show us around his house. Then we went up to look at Makoto's room.

Makoto still had a lot of boxes to unpack. He had some nice toys and kites. He said that on the next windy day, we could bring his kites outside and fly them. He said I could fly a kite by myself.

Then we went outside to look
at Makoto's pictures from Japan.
He had them in a green book.

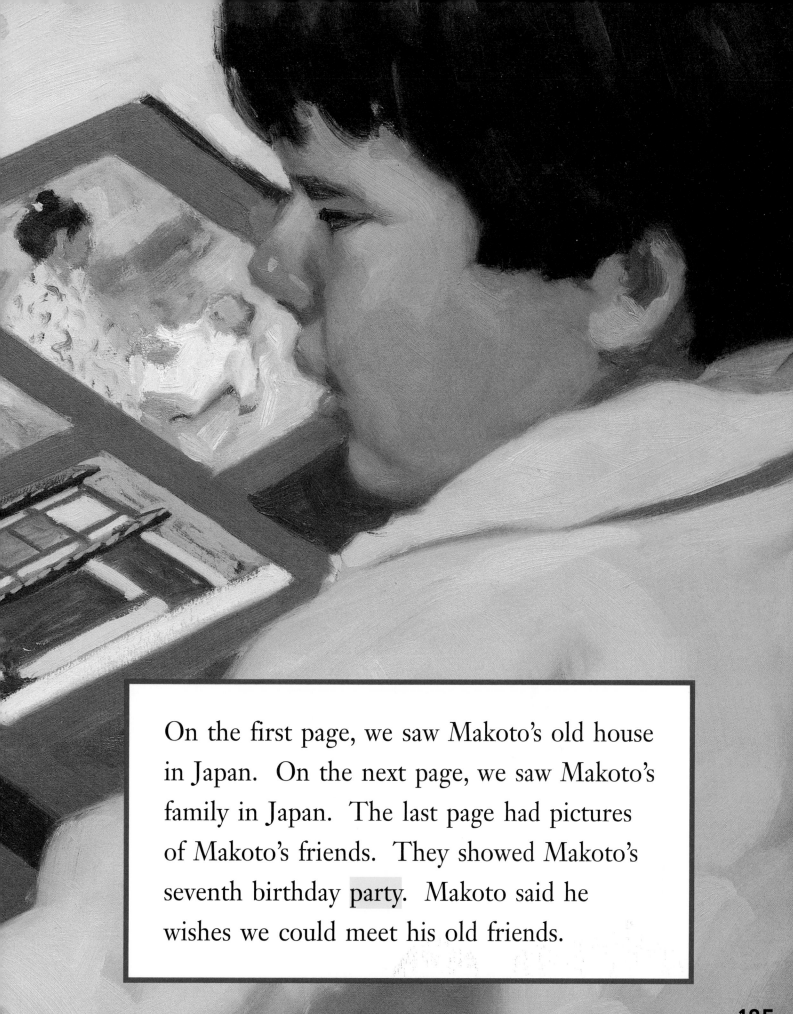

On the first page, we saw Makoto's old house in Japan. On the next page, we saw Makoto's family in Japan. The last page had pictures of Makoto's friends. They showed Makoto's seventh birthday party. Makoto said he wishes we could meet his old friends.

At the end of the day, Makoto's mother and
father repaid us for helping—with cookies!
We said "please" and "thank you" and ate up.

Makoto's father said he had a new job in the
city. Makoto would be going to our school.
We were all glad about that!

We said good-bye to Makoto and his mother and father. Then we went home to our families. We were glad to have a new friend next door.

Read Together

Your Turn

1. What is a <u>school</u>?

   ⬭ a place to learn

   ⬭ a place to sleep

   ⬭ a place to shop

   TEKS 1.3H, 1.6C

2. ✓ **TARGET SKILL** **Understanding Characters**
   How does Makoto feel about his new neighbors? How can you tell? **TEKS** 1.9B, 1.24C

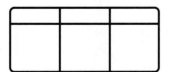

3. **Oral Language** Tell what happens in the beginning, middle, and end of the story. Use the Retelling Cards to help you. **TEKS** 1.4B, 1.9A, RC–1(E)

Retelling Cards

TEKS 1.3H identify/read high-frequency words; **1.4B** ask questions/seek clarification/locate details about texts; **1.6C** use syntax/context to determine meaning; **1.9A** retell story events; **1.9B** describe/analyze characters; **1.24C** record information in visual formats; **RC–1(E)** retell/act out important story events; **ELPS** **4G** demonstrate comprehension through shared reading/retelling/responding/note-taking

Dawn's
Voice
by Eileen Brady
illustrated by Tim Bowers

Dawn's Voice

by Eileen Brady

illustrated by Tim Bowers

Dawn had a nice voice.
Outside, her voice was loud.
Inside, her voice was soft.

At times, Dawn forgot which voice to use. If she forgot at home, Mom would say, "Use an inside voice, Dawn."

If she forgot at school, Miss Law
would whisper, "Too much noise.
How can we read? Use an inside
voice, Dawn."

Last week, Dawn was at a school game. Her school's Red Team led the game. The Yellow Team was at bat. The batter swung and hit hard.

Dawn shouted to Paul, "Look up, Paul! Look up!"

Dawn's loud voice filled the park. Would Paul hear it?

Paul did hear it. He looked up and made the catch. Dawn's team got the win.

With joy, Dawn joined the
school party. Paul thanked Dawn.
"My loud voice was just right!"
Dawn shouted. Then she said
with her soft voice, "Just right."

Neighborhoods

by Isabel Collins

Many people live, work, and go to school in a neighborhood. American cities have many neighborhoods. Two of these cities are San Francisco and Laredo. Where does your family live?

Cherry Blossom Festival in Japantown, San Francisco

San Francisco

Japantown is a neighborhood in the city of San Francisco. Many Japanese Americans live there.

Japantown has a Cherry Blossom Festival in the spring. It is like a big party. You can buy Japanese food and enjoy Japanese music, art, and dances.

United States

San Francisco

California

Texas

Laredo

Laredo

Many Mexican Americans live in the city of Laredo. It is called the "Gateway to Mexico." Laredo has had seven flags throughout history.

Each year there is a big festival to celebrate George Washington's birthday. There are pageants, concerts, and parades like this one. I like the Jalapeño Eating Contest, myself!

Save me some jalapeños, please!

Making Connections

Read Together

 Text to Self

TEKS RC-1(F)

Make a Map Make a map of your neighborhood that shows the places where you have fun.

 Text to Text

TEKS 1.27A, 1.28, 1.29

Talk About Neighborhoods With a partner, describe a place in a neighborhood where you would like to play. Listen to each other.

 Text to World

TEKS RC-1(F)

Connect to Social Studies What changes happen when people move to a new country? What stays the same? Describe to a partner what it might be like.

 TEKS **1.27A** listen attentively/ask relevant questions; **1.28** share information/ideas by speaking clearly; **1.29** follow discussion rules; **RC-1(F)** make connections to experiences/texts/community; **ELPS 2I** demonstrate listening comprehension of spoken English; **3H** narrate/describe/ explain with detail

Grammar
Read Together

Contractions A **contraction** is a short way of writing two words. This mark (') takes the place of missing letters.

It is a very big truck!
It's a very big truck!

He is helping his dad.
He's helping his dad.

This box is not too heavy.
This box **isn't** too heavy.

I do not know what is in it.
I **don't** know what is in it.

Write the contractions for the
underlined words. Use another
sheet of paper.

1. I am happy to meet a new friend.

2. Today he is moving next door.

3. Jamal is not finished unpacking.

4. I do not know what games he likes.

5. His toys are not on the shelves yet.

Grammar in Writing

When you proofread your writing, be sure
you have written contractions correctly.

Reading-Writing Workshop: Revise

Write to Express   Read Together

✔ **Sentence Fluency** A good **story** usually has some short sentences and some long ones.

Deval drafted a story about two friends. Later, he made a long sentence by joining two short sentences with **and**.

Revised Draft

Burt packed his six
,and
mittens. He got on a jet.

Revising Checklist

✔ Did I write some short and long sentences?

✔ Does my story have a beginning, a middle, and an end?

✔ Did I write the exact words a character says?

✔ Did I write contractions correctly?

204

Find short and long sentences in Deval's story. Use the Checklist to revise your draft.

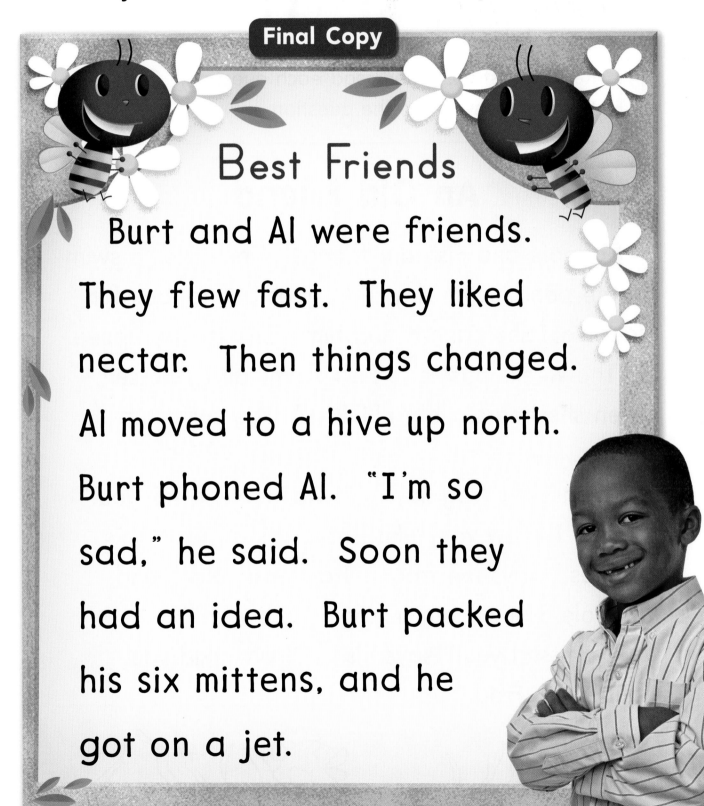

Final Copy

Best Friends

Burt and Al were friends. They flew fast. They liked nectar. Then things changed. Al moved to a hive up north. Burt phoned Al. "I'm so sad," he said. Soon they had an idea. Burt packed his six mittens, and he got on a jet.

Test POWER

Read the story. Then read each question. Choose the best answer for the question.

An Old Friend

Tadpole and Fish are friends. They like to swim in the pond. One day, Fish goes out to look for Tadpole. She cannot find him. She is very <u>upset</u>.

The weeks pass by. Fish swims all by herself. Then she hears a big PLOP! A frog swims up to her.

"Fish!" the frog says. "I was looking for you."

"Do I know you?" Fish asks.

"Yes," says the frog. "I am your old friend, Tadpole. Now I am a frog. I grew up!"

"I missed you!" says Fish. "I am glad you found me, Frog."

1   What does the word <u>upset</u> mean?

     ⬭ Nice

     ⬭ Sad

     ⬭ Happy

2   What happens to Tadpole?

     ⬭ He leaves the pond.

     ⬭ He does not like Fish anymore.

     ⬭ He changes into a frog.

3   How does Fish feel at the end?

     ⬭ Happy

     ⬭ Scared

     ⬭ Sad

GO ON ➡

Butterfly Visitors

Each fall, Monarch butterflies fly to Mexico for the winter. Many make stops in towns in Texas.

One town has a big party to <u>greet</u> the butterflies! People dress up in orange and black, the colors of the Monarchs. They sing and dance.

People also put tags on the butterflies when they stop by. This helps us learn more about the long trip each butterfly takes.

1   When do Monarchs fly to Mexico?
- ⬭ Summer
- ⬭ Winter
- ⬭ Fall

2   What does the word <u>greet</u> mean?
- ⬭ Welcome
- ⬭ Say goodbye
- ⬭ Warn

3   Why do the people wear orange and black?
- ⬭ To keep warm
- ⬭ To look like Monarch butterflies
- ⬭ To look like tigers

POWER Practice

TEKS 1.21A form letters legibly

Handwriting

Read Together

Be sure your words are spaced correctly.

correct

Max is my dog.

too close

Maxismydog.

too far apart

Max   is   my   dog.

TEKS 1.21A form letters legibly

Write these sentences on a sheet of paper. Use your best handwriting. Be sure to write uppercase and lowercase letters correctly. Use correct spacing.

Max runs fast.

I run after Max.

Max and I have fun.

TEKS 1.25 revise topic

Research Report

A research report answers a question about a topic. After you find information for a report, read your notes and think about them.

Rayna wanted to write a report about pet cats. She took notes. Then she circled the information she wanted to use in her report. Next, Rayna revised her topic. She decided to write about taking care of pet cats.

going to a vet

some cats walk on leash

dogs have to be walked

brushing cats

hard to give a bath

related to tigers and lions

Read these notes for a report on pet goldfish.

don't need heated water

biggest goldfish: 18 inches

sharks eat other fish

shouldn't try to pet goldfish

cats like to be petted

not all goldfish are gold

eat goldfish flakes

Talk with a partner. Answer these questions.

1. Which notes can be used in the report?

2. Does the report topic need to be revised?

Talk about the notes that you would use in a report about pet goldfish.

TEKS **1.6E** alphabetize/use dictionary; **1.22E** use resources to find correct spellings

Using a Dictionary

Read Together

A dictionary helps you find the meaning of a word. It also helps you check the spelling.

The words in a dictionary are in ABC order. Words that begin with the same letter are in the same part of a dictionary.

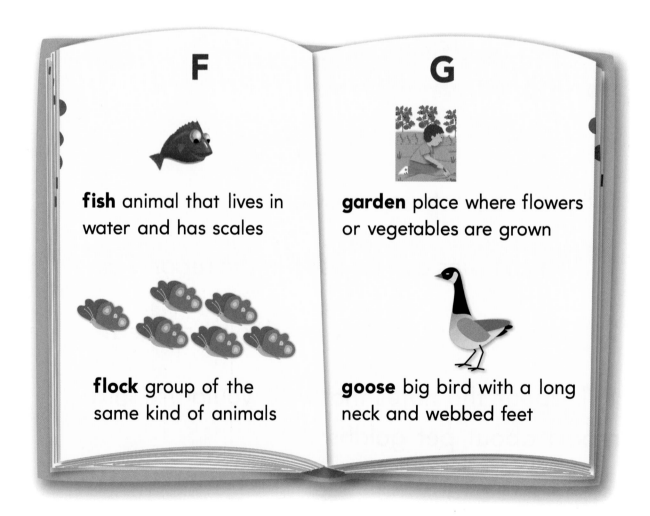

F

fish animal that lives in water and has scales

flock group of the same kind of animals

G

garden place where flowers or vegetables are grown

goose big bird with a long neck and webbed feet

Read each list of words. Which word would you find first in a dictionary? Write that word on a sheet of paper. Find it in a dictionary.

1. frog

hamster

elk

2. panda

goat

sheep

3. puppy

kitten

cub

4. camel

crane

chicken

5. toad

turtle

tiger

6. snake

shark

starfish

TEKS **1.6E** alphabetize/use dictionary; **1.21A** form letters legibly

ABC Order  Read Together

Knowing the alphabet can help you put words in ABC order.

A	B	C	D	E

Write these words on a sheet of paper.

joke   laugh   smile   funny   grin

Circle the first letter of each word. Use the first letter to write the words in ABC order. Write neatly from left to right.

216

Write these words on your paper.

friend   fast   flag   foot   first

These words all begin with the letter **f**. To put them in ABC order, you must look at the next letter. Circle the second letter in each word. Then write the words in ABC order. Remember to write neatly so others can read your work.

 **TEKS** 1.25 revise topic

Research Report

 Read Together

A research report answers a question about a topic. After you find information, it's time to start planning your report. You can begin by writing a short answer to your question.

Oscar wants to answer this question.

What do polar bears look like?

He reads his notes.

very large bear
white coat
big feet for walking on snow and ice

Then he writes a short answer to his question.

A polar bear is a very large bear with a white coat and big feet that help it walk on snow and ice.

Read the notes for a report about pandas.
Then write a sentence to answer this question.

What do pandas look like?

large bear

round face

white fur with black patches

Read your sentence to a partner.

TEKS 1.6D categorize words

Sorting Words

You can group words that are alike.

Family Members	Community Helpers	Places
sister	teacher	library
father	fire fighter	park

1. Make a chart like this one. Use another sheet of paper.

Family Members	Community Helpers	Places

2. Think about the words below. Some words belong on your chart and some do not.

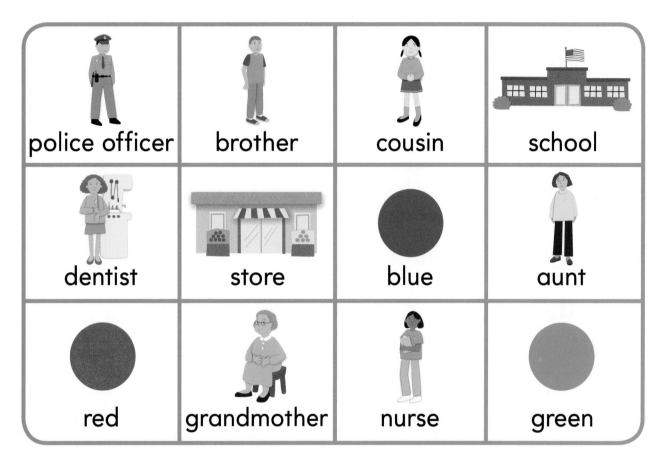

police officer	brother	cousin	school
dentist	store	blue	aunt
red	grandmother	nurse	green

3. Write the words in the right group on the chart.

4. Which words are left over? What group do they belong to?

Add more words to your chart.

TEKS 1.19B write short letters; 1.20A (vii) understand/use time-order transition words

Writing a Letter

You can write a letter to tell someone about something you've done. When you write a letter, make sure you have all the parts.

Heading ——————————————— April 7, 2010

Greeting — Dear Aunt Jo,

Body — Today Dad and I planted carrots. First, we dug little holes. Next, we put carrot seeds into the holes. Then we covered the seeds with dirt. Last, we watered the dirt. I can't wait to eat our carrots!

Closing ——————————————— Love,

Signature ——————————————— Nick

Write a letter to a family member. Tell them about something fun you did with a friend. Use words like **first, next, then,** and **last** to help tell the events in order. Remember to use the five parts of a letter. When you are finished, read your letter to a partner.

TEKS 1.21A form letters legibly

Handwriting  Read Together

Be sure your sentences are spaced correctly.

correct

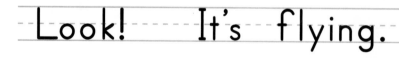

Look! It's flying.

too close

Look!It'sflying.

too far apart

Look!   It's flying.

Write these sentences on a sheet of paper.
Use your best handwriting. Use correct spacing.

Our kite is red. It is flying
high in the sky. Do you
like it?

TEKS **1.23A** generate topics/formulate questions; **1.25** revise topic

Revising a Topic

Read Together

A research report answers a question about a topic. Brainstorm with your classmates a list of topics that you find interesting. Choose a topic that you have a question about and find information. After you find information, start planning your report. If you have too much information, you can revise your research question.

Mimi wants to answer this question.

What do visitors see in big Texas cities?

She found facts about these cities.

Houston   **Dallas**

San Antonio   **Austin**

Mimi had too much information. She revised her research question.

What do visitors go to see in Austin, Texas?

Mack wanted to write a report on farm animals. This was his first research question.

Why do people raise farm animals?

Mack found facts about these animals.

cows	**sheep**
chickens	**goats**
horses	**pigs**

Write a new question Mack can use for his report. Share your question with a partner.

TEKS **1.4B** ask questions/seek clarification/locate details about texts; **1.20C** ask questions with subject-verb inversion

Asking Questions

When you ask a question, a question word or a verb often comes first. The answer may have the same words in a different order.

Questions	Answers
What **is** the snake's **name**?	The snake's **name is** Snoop.
Is Snoop asleep?	**Snoop is** wide awake.
Can Snoop wiggle?	**Snoop can** wiggle a lot!
Will Snoop move soon?	**Snoop will** move in a while.

Look at the pictures below. Write two questions about the pets. Be sure your words are in an order that makes sense. Trade papers with a partner. Write answers to your partner's questons.

TEKS 1.21A form letters legibly

Handwriting

Be sure your sentences are spaced correctly.

correct

Let's race. Go!

too close

Let'sraceGo!

too far apart

Let's race. Go!

Write these sentences on a sheet of paper. Use your best handwriting. Use correct spacing.

We like to run. We can all go fast. Who will win the race?

Read your sentences to a partner.

TEKS 1.23B determine relevant sources of information

Determine Sources

Read Together

A research report answers a question about a topic. After you find information for a report, read your notes and think about them. You might decide that you need more information.

Pedro is planning a report about bluebonnets. He has these notes.

state flower of Texas

bright blue flowers

grow about 1 foot tall

planted by highways in Texas

Pedro wants another fact for his report. He wants to know when bluebonnets bloom. He looks in an encyclopedia. Then he adds a note.

bloom in April and May

Read these notes for a report on mockingbirds.

state bird of Texas

about 10 inches long

eat bugs and seeds

build nests in trees

Talk with a partner. Answer these questions.

1. Do the notes tell about the color of mockingbirds?

2. Where could you look for another fact about mockingbirds?

TEKS **1.17E** publish/share writing

Publishing

After you wrote your story, you revised it. Now you are ready to share your story with the rest of your class.

One way to share a story is to write a neat final copy. Then you can draw a picture to go with your story.

Benny the Bee

Work with a group. Talk about each person's story. Be sure there are some long sentences and some short sentences. Talk about a picture that could go with each story.

After your discussion, write a neat copy of your story. Ask a partner to read your story to be sure you copied it correctly. Then draw a picture to go with your story.

Put your story and your picture up in the classroom. Let your classmates read your story and look at your picture.

Read your classmates' stories. Tell one good thing about each story.

TEKS 1.15B explain signs/symbols

Signs and Symbols

Read Together

Remember that signs can use shapes, pictures, and words to tell about something or tell what something is.

On a separate sheet of paper, write what these signs probably tell.

1.

CATTLE XING

2.

CLOSED

3.

SLOW

4.

5.

6.

7.

8. BACK IN
10
MINUTES

Make a sign you would like
to put up in your classroom.

TEKS **1.21A** form letters legibly; **1.22C** spell high-frequency words

Spelling

Read Together

Read the words below. Then answer the questions on another sheet of paper.

also	ready	buy	please
kind	seven	city	school
anything	warm	family	places

1. Which four words end in **y**?

2. Which two words begin like **plant**?

3. Which word means **nice**?

4. Which word is the opposite of **cool**?

Words to Know

Unit 5   High-Frequency Words

21 "The Tree"

told	thought
night	better
pretty	turned
window	saw

22 Amazing Animals

learning	young
begins	follow
until	years
eight	baby

23 Whistle for Willie

house	father
along	again
together	nothing
boy	began

24 A Butterfly Grows

ready	places
anything	also
upon	flower
kind	warm

25 The New Friend

city	seven
myself	buy
school	please
party	family

Glossary

A

amazing

Something **amazing** will cause surprise. It is **amazing** to see a shooting star.

awful

Awful means very bad or terrible. I had an **awful** pain in my side, so I went to the doctor.

B

beautiful

Beautiful means nice to see or hear. The garden was full of **beautiful** flowers.

brushes

A **brush** is a tool that is used for scrubbing. We use the **brushes** to scrub the floors.

butterfly

A **butterfly** is an insect that has four wings. The **butterfly** flew from flower to flower.

C

camel

A **camel** is a large animal with a long neck and one or two humps. We saw a **camel** at the animal park.

carton

A **carton** is a box used to store things. Martin packed his toys in the **carton** before he moved.

caterpillar

A **caterpillar** is an insect shaped like a worm. This **caterpillar** will change into a butterfly.

chrysalis

A **chrysalis** is a stage that butterflies go through. The butterfly broke out of the **chrysalis** and stretched its wings.

color

A **color** is a kind of light that comes from an object to our eyes. Green is my favorite **color**.

crates

A **crate** is a kind of box used for packing things.
We packed the books in **crates** to move them.

crew

A **crew** is a group of people who work together.
The **crew** worked together to build the ship.

D

delivery

Delivery is a way of bringing something to someone.
When our school ordered the books, the **delivery**
was quick.

dolphin

A **dolphin** is a sea animal related to a whale. The
dolphin swam next to the ship.

drooped

To **droop** means to sag or hang loosely. The flower
drooped when it didn't get any water.

E

empty

Empty means with nothing inside. When I opened the box, it was **empty**.

errand

An **errand** is a special trip you take to do something. I ran an **errand** for my mom.

G

grocery

A **grocery** store is where you buy food. Luke stopped at the **grocery** store to pick up some bread for dinner.

H

happened

To **happen** means to take place. Mr. Chow read about what **happened** in the park.

L

lemonade
Lemonade is a drink made from lemons.
I like to drink **lemonade** on a hot day.

llama
A **llama** is an animal that looks like
a camel. My aunt has a pet **llama**
on her ranch.

M

milkweed
Milkweed is a kind of plant with a white juice. Monarch
caterpillars eat **milkweed** leaves.

monarch
A **monarch** is a kind of butterfly. A **monarch** butterfly
has orange, black, and white wings.

P

pails

A **pail** is something you use to carry things. The people used **pails** to carry water to put out the fire.

pleased

Pleased means to be made happy. Ms. Perez was **pleased** when her students did so well.

pocket

A **pocket** is a small bag of cloth. I always keep my money in the **pocket** of my pants.

polar bear

A **polar bear** is a large white bear that lives where it is cold. A **polar bear** will roll in the snow to clean its fur.

porcupine

A **porcupine** is an animal that is covered with long sharp quills. Most animals will leave a **porcupine** alone.

R

rejoined

To **rejoin** means to get together again. We **rejoined** the group after we finished our chores.

repaid

To **repay** means to give something back. I **repaid** my brother for the money he loaned me.

S

seventh

If something is **seventh**, that means that there are six things before it. Saturday is the **seventh** day of the week.

shadow

A **shadow** is a dark area with light around it. The sun made a **shadow** behind the tree.

soccer

Soccer is a game where players kick a ball. Nina was a very good **soccer** player because she was fast.

staked

To **stake** means to use a pointed stick to help something stand up. Andrea **staked** the plant to help it grow straight.

stroked

To **stroke** means to rub gently. Matt **stroked** the puppy to make it calm down.

T

themselves

Themselves means those people or animals. As animals get older, they can take care of **themselves**.

toes

Toes are the parts of the foot that help people and other animals walk. People have five **toes** on each foot.

U

unloaded

To **unload** means to take off. The woman **unloaded** the bags of food from the car.

unpack

To **unpack** means to take out of a box or a suitcase. We started to **unpack** the boxes in the kitchen.

W

whirled

To **whirl** means to spin or to turn in circles. My little brother **whirled** and whirled until he was dizzy.

Acknowledgments

"Caballito blanco, reblanco/Little White Horse" from *Mamá Goose: A Latino Nursery Treasury* by Alma Flor Ada and F. Isabel Campoy. Text copyright © 2004 by Alma Flor Ada and F. Isabel Campoy. Reprinted by permission of Hyperion Books for Children. All rights reserved.

The New Friend, originally published as *El Amigo Nuevo* by Maria Puncel, illustrated by Ulises Wensell. Copyright © 1995 Laredo Publishing Company. Reprinted by permission of Laredo Publishing Company, Inc.

"Pet Snake" by Rebecca Kai Dotlich from *A Pet For Me*, published by HarperCollins. Copyright © 2003 by Rebecca Kai Dotlich. Reprinted by permission of Curtis Brown, Ltd.

"The Tree" from *Poppleton Forever* by Cynthia Rylant, illustrated by Mark Teague. Text copyright © 1998 by Cynthia Rylant. Illustrations copyright © 1998 by Mark Teague. All rights reserved. Reprinted by permission of Blue Sky Press, a division of Scholastic, Inc.

Whistle for Willie by Ezra Jack Keats. Copyright © 1964 by Ezra Jack Keats. All rights reserved including the right of reproduction in whole or in part in any form. Reprinted by permission of Viking Children's Books, a member of Penguin Young Readers Group, a division of Penguin Group (USA), Inc.

Credits

Photo Credits

Placement Key: (t) top, (b) bottom, (r) right, (l) left, (bg) background, (fg) foreground, (i) inset

TOC 8a ©Michael S. Quinton/Getty Images; **TOC 8b** ©Scott Nielsen/Bruce Coleman USA; **9** ©Michael S. Quinton/Getty images; **10** (t) ©Gary Crabbe/Alamy; (b) ©Gail Jankus/Photo Researchers, Inc.; **11** (tl) ©imagebroker/Alamy; (tr) ©Mark Bolton/Corbis; (cl) ©John Henley/ Corbis; (inset) ©Siede Preis/Photodisc; (cr) ©Omni Photo Communications Inc./IndexStock; (bl) ©Comstock /SuperStock; (br) ©Scott Barrow/ Corbis; **12** ©Gary W. Carter/Corbis; **13** Katrina Brown/Alamy; **14** ©Courtesy of Cynthia Rylant; ©Courtesy of Mark Teague; **40** (inset) ©Corbis/ SuperStock; **40-41** (bgd) ©Getty Images; **41** (inset) ©Corbis; **42** (inset) ©Niels-DK/Alamy; **43** (br) ©Stockbyte; (br) PhotoDisc; **48** (t) ©A & M SHAH/Animals Animals - Earth Scenes; (b) ©Joe McDonald/Corbis; **49** (tl) ©Steve Maslowski/Visuals Unlimited/Getty Images; (tr) ©blickwinkel/Alamy; (cl) ©Beverly Joubert/ National Geographic/Getty Images; (cr) ©Gavriel Jecan/ Photographer's Choice/Getty Images; **50** (bl) ©DLILLC/Corbis; (br) © Keren Su/ China Span/Alamy; (tr) ©Chase Swift/Corbis; (br) ©Kevin Schafer/Corbis; (bl) ©Gallo Images/ Corbis; (tl) ©ChinaFotoPress/Getty Images News/Getty Images; (tl) ©G.K. & Vikki Hart; **52** ©Hmco/John Lei; **84** ©EyeWire; ©Ariel Skelley/Riser/Getty Images; **85** ©1996 PhotoDisc, Inc. All rights reserved. Images provided by © 1996 CMCD; **88** (t) ©Dennis Lane/Index Stock Imagery/Jupiter Images; (b) ©Davis Barber/ PhotoEdit; **89** (tl) ©Image Source/Corbis; (tr) ©Tony Freeman/PhotoEdit; (cl) ©Tom Grill/ Corbis; (cr) ©LWA/Dann Tardif/Getty Images; (bl) ©Bubbles Photolibrary/Alamy; (br) ©Somos Images/Corbis; **90** ©Dorling Kindersley/ Getty Images; **92** ©Courtesy of Ezra Jack Keats; **125** Gandee Vasan/Getty Images; **127** ©B.Bird/zefa/Corbis; **130** ©Naturfoto Honal/ Corbis; ©Superstudio/The Imagebank/Getty